# The Yogurt Cookbook That Will Absolutely Amaze You

## The Best Yoghurt Recipes That Everyone Will Love

BY: Allie Allen

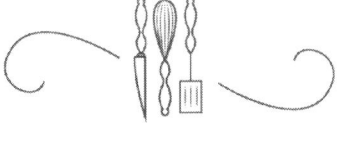

Copyright 2019 Allie Allen

# Copyright Notes

This book is written as an informational tool. While the author has taken every precaution to ensure the accuracy of the information provided therein, the reader is warned that they assume all risk when following the content. The author will not be held responsible for any damages that may occur as a result of the readers' actions.

The author does not give permission to reproduce this book in any form, including but not limited to: print, social media posts, electronic copies or photocopies, unless permission is expressly given in writing.

# Table of Contents

Delicious Yoghurt Recipes ........................................................... 6

Chapter I: Smoothies ................................................................. 7

    1) Peach Smoothie ................................................................ 8

    2) Vanilla Malt Smoothie ..................................................... 10

    3) Green Tea Yogurt Smoothie ........................................... 11

    4) Pina Colada Yogurt Smoothie ........................................ 13

    5) Chocolate and Fruit Smoothie ....................................... 15

Chapter II: Breakfasts ............................................................. 17

    6) Veggie Frittata .............................................................. 18

    7) Yogurt Parfait ............................................................... 20

    8) French Toast Casserole ................................................. 23

    9) Banana and Peanut Butter Oatmeal .............................. 25

    10) Oatmeal and Yogurt Pancake ...................................... 27

Chapter III: Lunches ............................................................... 29

11) Carrot and Raisin Salad ................................................ 30

12) Cucumber Soup ......................................................... 32

13) Creamy Mac and Cheese with Bacon........................... 34

14) Waldorf Yogurt Salad .................................................. 37

15) Chicken and Mashed Potatoes for Lunch ..................... 39

Chapter IV: Dinners............................................................. 41

16) Stroganoff made with Beef .......................................... 42

17) Garlic Buttered Tilapia ................................................ 45

18) Chicken Crusted in Almonds ....................................... 47

19) Vegetarian Casserole.................................................... 49

20) Zesty Mushroom Pork Chops....................................... 51

Chapter V: Desserts ............................................................. 55

21) Vanilla Frozen Yogurt.................................................. 56

22) Yogurt and Cream Cheese Frosting .............................. 58

23) Deliciously Light Cheesecake ...................................... 60

24) Carrot Yogurt Cake ...................................................... 62

25) White Chocolate Brownies ........................................... 65

About the Author................................................................. 67

Author's Afterthoughts........................................................ 69

# Delicious Yoghurt Recipes

sssssssssssssssssssssssssssssssssssssssssssssss

# Chapter I: Smoothies

sssssssssssssssssssssssssssssssssssssssssss

# 1) Peach Smoothie

Who doesn't love the taste of a juicy peach? And when you add it to a yogurt smoothie, you get a delicious and comforting beverage that you can enjoy on a warm summer evening.

**Yield:** 1 to 2

**Cooking Time:** 10 to 20 minutes

**List of Ingredients:**

- 1 ½ cups vanilla Greek yogurt
- 1 banana, peeled and sliced
- 8 ounces strawberries, stems removed
- ¾ cup peaches, skin removed and diced
- 1 tbsp. concentrate orange juice

sssssssssssssssssssssssssssssssssssssssssssss

**Procedure:**

**1:** Place all the ingredients into a blender. Turn the blender on high and blend the ingredients until they develop a creamy and smooth consistency.

**2:** Pour the smoothie into the desired drinking glass and enjoy.

# 2) Vanilla Malt Smoothie

This yogurt smoothie has a flavor reminiscent of the malted milkshakes of days past.

**Yield:** 1 to 2

**Cooking Time:** 10 to 20 minutes

**List of Ingredients:**

- ½ cup Greek yogurt
- 1 tbsp. malted milk extract
- 1 cup milk, soy
- ½ cup ice cubes

**Procedure:**

**1:** Place all the ingredients into a blender. Turn the blender on high and blend the ingredients until they develop a creamy and smooth consistency.

**2:** Pour the smoothie into the desired drinking glass and enjoy.

# 3) Green Tea Yogurt Smoothie

In recent years, the popularity of green tea has soared so it's only natural to incorporate it into a yogurt smoothie.

**Yield:** 1 to 2 serving

**Cooking Time:** 15 to 30 minutes

**List of Ingredients:**

- 1 cup green tea, strongly brewed
- 1/3 cup Greek yogurt
- 1 frozen banana, peeled and sliced
- 1 cup fresh baby spinach
- ½ cup berries
- 1 to 2 tsp. honey

sssssssssssssssssssssssssssssssssssssssssssss

**Procedure:**

**1:** Place all the ingredients into a blender. Turn the blender on high and blend the ingredients until they develop a creamy and smooth consistency.

**2:** Pour the smoothie into the desired drinking glass and enjoy.

# 4) Pina Colada Yogurt Smoothie

This delicious coconut and pineapple smoothie will transport you to a tropical getaway with one sip.

**Yield:** 1 to 2

**Cooking Time:** 10 to 20 minutes

**List of Ingredients:**

- ¼ cup vanilla Greek yogurt
- ¼ cup coconut milk
- 1 cup pineapple, cubed
- 1 tbsp. coconut flakes, sweetened
- 4 ice cubes

sssssssssssssssssssssssssssssssssssssssssssss

**Procedure:**

**1:** Place all the ingredients into a blender. Turn the blender on high and blend the ingredients until they develop a creamy and smooth consistency.

**2:** Pour the smoothie into the desired drinking glass and enjoy.

# 5) Chocolate and Fruit Smoothie

This delicious yogurt smoothie gives you the perfect combination of chocolate and fruit.

**Yield:** 1 to 2

**Cooking Time:** 10 to 20 minutes

**List of Ingredients:**

- 1 cup strawberries, stems removed
- 2 frozen bananas, peeled and sliced
- 1 cup Greek yogurt, low-fat
- 2 tbsp. milk chocolate, shavings

sssssssssssssssssssssssssssssssssssssssssssss

**Procedure:**

**1:** Place all the ingredients into a blender. Turn the blender on high and blend the ingredients until they develop a creamy and smooth consistency.

**2:** Pour the smoothie into the desired drinking glass and enjoy.

# Chapter II: Breakfasts

sssssssssssssssssssssssssssssssssssssssssss

# 6) Veggie Frittata

Both flavorful and fluffy, this veggie frittata contains eggs and Greek yogurt to make a protein-filled breakfast.

**Yield:** 4

**Cooking Time:** 25 to 30 minutes

**List of Ingredients:**

- 6 egg whites
- 3 whole eggs
- ¾ cup Asiago cheese, shredded
- ½ cup Greek yogurt, nonfat
- 1 minced garlic clove
- 1 tbsp. olive oil
- ½ cup bell pepper, chopped
- 4 cups baby spinach, fresh and torn into small pieces
- 1 cup mushrooms, sliced
- ¼ tsp. ground pepper
- ¼ tsp. table salt
- 1 tbsp. fresh basil leaves, torn into small pieces
- 1 tbsp. parmesan cheese, grated

sss

**Procedure:**

**1:** Turn the broiler on and let preheat. Whisk the egg whites, whole eggs, Asiago cheese and yogurt together. Set the mixture to the side for the moment.

**2:** Pour the olive oil into a skillet (oven-proof) and set on the stove over medium heat. Add the onion and garlic and sauté until the onions are translucent, which should take about 3 minutes.

**3:** Stir in the red pepper, spinach, mushrooms, basil, pepper and salt. Let cook for about 4 minutes.

**4:** Turn the heat down to low. Pour the egg mixture into the skillet and cover. Let cook for about 6 minutes.

**5:** Add the Parmesan cheese over the cooked mixture before setting the skillet into the broiler for about 3 minutes.

**6:** Remove the skillet from the broiler and let cook for about 5 minutes before serving.

# 7) Yogurt Parfait

This parfait recipe features yogurt and quinoa granola to create a delicious and healthy breakfast.

**Yield:** 4

**Cooking Time:** 25 to 30 minutes

**List of Ingredients:**

**Granola:**

- 1 cup buck wheat groats
- 1 cup oats, whole-rolled
- 1/3 cup quinoa
- ¾ cups almonds, chopped
- ¼ cup walnuts, chopped
- ¼ cup pumpkin seeds
- 2 tbsp. chia seeds, ground
- ¼ cup sunflower seeds
- ½ cup coconut, shredded and unsweetened
- 1 tsp. allspice
- 1 tsp. ginger, ground
- 2 tsp. cinnamon
- 1/3 cup dried cranberries, unsweetened
- 1/3 cup dates, chopped
- 2 tbsp. unsweetened apricots, chopped
- ½ cup pure maple syrup
- ¼ cup melted coconut oil

**Parfait:**

- 4 cup plain Greek yogurt, nonfat and plain
- 1 cup chopped fruit or mixed berries

sssssssssssssssssssssssssssssssssssssssssssss

**Procedure:**

**1:** Turn the oven on to 225-degrees. Mix all the ingredients for the granola together. Line a baking sheet with wax paper and spread the granola mixture onto the lined baking sheet. Set the baking sheet in the oven and bake for 60 minutes. Remove from the oven and let cool before crumbling the granola.

**2:** Assemble each parfait by spooning ½ cup of Greek yogurt into each of the 4 glasses. Add 1 tbsp. of the granola and then 2 tbsp. of the fruit. Repeat the process again for a second layer. Serve immediately.

## 8) French Toast Casserole

This delicious breakfast casserole is made the night before and then baked in the morning.

**Yield:** 8

**Cooking Time:** 40 to 50 minutes

**List of Ingredients:**

- 1 loaf bread, stale
- 2 egg whites
- 5 whole eggs
- 1 cup Greek yogurt, vanilla nonfat
- 1 cup milk, low fat
- ¾ cup maple syrup, pure
- 2 tbsp. butter, cold and diced
- 1/3 cup packed brown sugar
- 1 tsp. cinnamon
- ¼ cup flour, all-purpose
- ¼ cup pecans, minced (optional)

sssssssssssssssssssssssssssssssssssssssssssss

**Procedure:**

**1:** Coat the bottom of the 9x13 casserole dish with cooking spray. Tear the stale bread into pieces. Layer the pieces along the bottom of the dish.

**2:** In a large mixing bowl, whisk the egg white, whole eggs, low-fat milk, Greek yogurt and maple syrup together until smooth. Pour this mixture over the bread pieces from Step 1.

**3:** In a second mixing bowl, mix the cinnamon, brown sugar, butter, pecans and flour together. Continue mixing until well combined but a little lumpy.

**4:** Sprinkle the mixture from Step 3 over the bread. Cover the dish and place in the fridge overnight.

**5:** The next morning, start the baking process by preheating the oven to 350-degrees. Set the dish in the oven and bake for about 45-minutes. You want the middle to be set and the top to be golden brown.

**6:** Serve while still warm. Top with maple syrup.

# 9) Banana and Peanut Butter Oatmeal

This delicious yogurt breakfast recipe can be made now or the night before.

**Yield:** 8

**Cooking Time:** 40 to 45 minutes

**List of Ingredients:**

- 2 cups oats
- ¼ tsp. baking powder
- ¼ tsp. baking soda
- ½ tsp. cinnamon
- ¼ cup flaxseed, ground
- ¾ cup Greek yogurt, nonfat and plain
- 2 ripe bananas, peeled and sliced
- 1 cup almond milk, unsweetened
- 1 egg, lightly beaten
- ¼ cup peanut butter
- ¼ cup pure maple syrup

sss

**Procedure:**

**1:** Lightly coat a 1.5-quart dish with cooking spray.

**2:** Combine all the dry ingredients together in a mixing bowl. Set the bowl to the side for the moment.

**3:** In a second mixing bowl, combine all the wet ingredients together. Carefully pour the wet mixture into the dry mixture and mix until well combined.

**4:** Transfer the mixture into the baking dish from Step 1. Cover the dish and set in the fridge until ready to use.

**5:** When ready to bake, place in an oven preheated to 350-degrees and bake for about 30 minutes. Serve warm.

# 10) Oatmeal and Yogurt Pancake

These light and fluffy pancakes are made with oatmeal and yogurt for a delicious pancake that is much healthier than their boxed counterparts.

**Yield:** about 15 pancakes

**Cooking Time:** 25 to 30 minutes

**List of Ingredients:**

- 1 cup vanilla Greek yogurt, nonfat
- 1 cup milk, low-fat
- 2 eggs
- 1 cup oats
- 1 cup flour, whole-wheat
- 1 tsp. baking soda
- 1 tsp. baking powder
- 1 tsp. sugar, turbinado
- ½ tsp. cinnamon
- ¼ tsp. salt
- 1 tsp. maple syrup, 100-percent pure

sss

**Procedure:**

**1:** Combine the yogurt, milk and eggs together until smooth. Stir in the oats, flours, baking soda, baking powder, sugar, cinnamon, salt and maple syrup. Continue to mix until the ingredients are well combined.

**2:** Apply nonstick cooking spray to the bottom of a large skillet. Place the skillet on the stove and set over medium heat.

**3:** Pour the batter into the heated skillet to form pancake shapes. Cook each pancake until bubbles begin to form in the batter. Flip the pancakes over and cook the other side. Continue in this manner until all the batter is used.

**4:** Serve the pancakes warm with maple syrup or the desired toppings.

# Chapter III: Lunches

sssssssssssssssssssssssssssssssssssssssssss

# 11) Carrot and Raisin Salad

This delicious salad is perfect when you want something a bit different for lunch.

**Yield:** 1 to 2

**Cooking Time:** 25 to 30 minutes + 1 to 2 hours to chill

**List of Ingredients:**

- 4 cups carrots, shredded
- ½ cup toasted pecans, chopped
- 1 can crushed pineapple; juice drained but reserved
- ¼ cup plain Greek yogurt
- ¼ cup raisins
- 1 tsp. granulated sugar
- Pinch of table salt

**Procedure:**

**1:** In a mixing bowl, combined the carrots, crushed pineapple, pecans and raisins.

**2:** In a second mixing bowl, mix 2 ½ tbsp. of the pineapple juice, yogurt, sugar and salt.

**3:** Transfer the yogurt mixture to the bowl from Step 1 and stir. Cover the bowl and place in the fridge for a few hours. Serve chilled.

# 12) Cucumber Soup

This refreshing soup is light and perfect for those summer days. For best flavor, make the soup the night before.

**Yield:** 4

**Cooking Time:** 20 to 25 minutes + chill over night

**List of Ingredients:**

- 2 cucumbers, peeled and diced
- 1 cup Greek yogurt, plain and nonfat
- 2 cups buttermilk, reduced fat
- 2 tsp. table or kosher salt
- Juice from a lemon
- Rind from half a lemon, minced
- ½ cup chives, snipped into small pieces
- 2/3 tbsp. dill weed
- Ground black pepper

ssssssssssssssssssssssssssssssssssssssssssssssss

**Procedure:**

**1:** Place all the ingredients in a ceramic bowl and stir together until well blended. Place the mixture in the fridge to chill overnight.

**2:** Serve the soup chilled.

# 13) Creamy Mac and Cheese with Bacon

This delicious recipe uses yogurt to create a creamy dish and includes bacon to kick the traditional mac and cheese up a notice.

**Yield:** 6

**Cooking Time:** 40 to 50 minutes

**List of Ingredients:**

- 2 cups elbow macaroni, uncooked
- 2 tbsp. flour, all-purpose
- 2 tbsp. butter
- ½ tsp. black pepper, ground
- ½ tsp. table salt
- ¼ cup Greek yogurt, plain and nonfat
- 1 ½ cup milk, fat-free
- 5 ounces fontina cheese, shredded
- 1 cup cheddar cheese, shredded
- 1 tbsp. Parmesan cheese, grated
- 1 tbsp. bread crumbs
- 4 slices cooked bacon

sssssssssssssssssssssssssssssssssssssssssssss

**Procedure:**

**1:** Preheat an oven to 400-degrees. Prepare a 1 ½-quart baking dish by buttering the bottom and the sides.

**2:** Cook the pasta as directed on the package until it is al dente. Drain the pasta and set to the side for the moment.

**3:** Melt the butter in a small saucepan. Stir in the pepper, salt and flour. Mix together until the ingredients are smooth. Stir in the milk and yogurt until smooth. Add the cheddar cheese and fontina cheese and melt. You want the mixture to be smooth yet thick.

**4:** Pour the cheese mixture from Step 3 into a mixing bowl. Add the cooked pasta and stir until the pasta is well covered with the cheese mixture.

**5:** Transfer the cheese-covered pasta into the prepared baking dish. Sprinkle the Parmesan cheese and bread crumbs on top. Crumble the bacon over the dish.

**6:** Place the baking dish in the oven and bake for 25 minutes. Serve warm.

# 14) Waldorf Yogurt Salad

Salads make an easy and delicious lunch that can be made the night before.

**Yield:** 1

**Cooking Time:** 25 to 30 minutes

**List of Ingredients:**

- ½ cup Greek yogurt
- 2 tsp. mayonnaise
- 2 tbsp. + 2 tsp. lemon juice
- ½ tsp. cumin, ground
- ¾ tsp. curry powder
- ¼ tsp. salt
- 2 Fuji apples, cored and cut into wedges
- 1 cup celery, sliced
- 1/3 cup walnut halves, toasted
- ¼ cup parsley, chopped
- ¼ cup raisins

ssssssssssssssssssssssssssssssssssssssssssssss

**Procedure:**

**1:** Mix the yogurt, mayonnaise, 2 tbsp. lemon juice, curry powder, cumin and salt together. Set this dressing to the side.

**2:** Place the apple wedges into a mixing bowl. Add the remaining 2 tbsp. of lemon juice and toss until well coated.

**3:** Add the raisins, walnuts and celery to the bowl with the lemon juice-covered apples and mix until combined.

**4:** Transfer the dressing from Step 1 to the mixing bowl and mix until the ingredients are coated.

**5:** Serve with parsley. If desired, season with ground black pepper and table salt to taste.

# 15) Chicken and Mashed Potatoes for Lunch

This delicious lunch recipe uses yogurt to create a creamy mash potato dish that is both yummy and filling.

**Yield:** 1 to 2

**Cooking Time:** 35 to 40 minutes

**List of Ingredients:**

- 1 cooked chicken breast
- 1 large potato, russet
- 1 ½ tbsp. olive oil
- 2 tbsp. salted butter
- ¼ cup half and half
- ¼ cup Greek yogurt, plain
- 1 tbsp. chives, chopped
- ½ garlic clove, minced finely
- Salt and pepper to taste

**Procedure:**

**1:** Clean the potato and prick it with a fork several times. Place the potato into a microwave-safe glass dish. Add about an inch of water to the dish and cook in the microwave for 10 to 12 minutes.

**2:** Place the cooked potato into a large bowl and mash roughly. Add the olive oil, butter, yogurt, chives and garlic and mash until well incorporated.

**3:** Using a hand mixer, whip the ingredients together until creamy and smooth. Add the half and half a little at a time. Season to taste with salt and pepper.

**4:** Serve the mashed potatoes with the cooked chicken.

# Chapter IV: Dinners

ssssssssssssssssssssssssssssssssssssssssssss

## 16) Stroganoff made with Beef

This recipe takes the classic dish and improves it with the added flavor of Greek yogurt.

**Yield:** 6

**Cooking Time:** 25 to 30 minutes

**List of Ingredients:**

- 2 tbsp. olive oil
- 1 onion, chopped
- 8 ounces mushrooms (button variety), cleaned and stems removed
- 1 tsp. dried mustard
- 2 garlic cloves, minced
- 2 tbsp. + ¼ cup flour, whole wheat
- Ground pepper, to taste
- Salt, to taste
- 1 ½ cups beef broth
- 1 tsp. Worcestershire sauce
- 1 cup red wine (dry)
- 2 tbsp. butter, unsalted
- 2 pounds filet mignon, cubed into bite-size pieces
- 2 tbsp. fresh dill weed
- 1 cup Greek yogurt, plain and nonfat

sssssssssssssssssssssssssssssssssssssssssssssss

**Procedure:**

**1:** Add the oil to a large pan and heat over medium heat. Sauté the mushrooms, garlic and onion for about 5 minutes.

**2:** Stir in the salt, mustard, pepper and 2 tbsp. flour. Add the beef broth and continue to stir until the mixture has thickened. Pour the Worcestershire and wine into the skillet. Let the mixture boil before turning the heat off.

**3:** Cover the counter with wax paper. Sprinkle the remaining ¼ cup flour across the wax paper and roll the filet mignon pieces in it until well coated.

**4:** Melt the butter in a sauce pan. Place the filet mignon pieces in the pan and let sear for 1 minute.

**5:** Place the beef in the mushroom mixture. Stir in the dill weed until well mixed. Simmer this mixture in the pan for about 15 minutes. Add the yogurt and stir.

**6:** Serve over noodles, rice or quinoa.

# 17) Garlic Buttered Tilapia

This fish dish is easy to prepare but will seem like you spent all day preparing the meal.

**Yield:** 4

**Cooking Time:** 45 – 55 minutes

**List of Ingredients:**

- 1-pound tilapia filets
- 2 tbsp. butter, salted or unsalted
- 2 garlic cloves, minced
- 1 onion, diced
- ½ cup Greek yogurt, plain and nonfat
- 1 tbsp. lemon juice
- Parsley for garnish (optional)

sssssssssssssssssssssssssssssssssssssssssssssss

**Procedure:**

**1:** Turn the oven to 350-degrees and let preheat.

**2:** Add the butter, garlic and onion in a skillet. Place on the stove and cook over medium heat for 4 minutes. Transfer half of the mixture into a 9x13 baking dish. Spread the mixture evenly along the bottom of the baking dish.

**3:** Add the other half of the butter mixture to a small mixing bowl. Add the lemon juice and yogurt and stir until well combined.

**4:** Position the tilapia filets in the baking dish, laying them on top of the butter mixture. Spread the yogurt/butter mixture on top of the filets.

**5:** Place the baking dish in the oven and bake for about 30 minutes. You want the fish to flake when forked. Place the parsley along the side of the fish and serve immediately.

# 18) Chicken Crusted in Almonds

This chicken recipe is baked not fried to give you a crispy and healthier dinner dish that is light and tasty.

**Yield:** 6

**Cooking Time:** 45 to 50 minutes

**List of Ingredients:**

- 6 chicken breasts, skinless and boneless
- 2 tbsp. almonds, slivered or sliced
- ½ cup Greek yogurt, plain and nonfat
- 2 large eggs
- ½ tsp. dried oregano
- ¼ tsp. onion powder
- ¼ tsp. garlic powder
- ¼ tsp. ground black pepper
- 1/8 tsp. kosher or table salt
- ½ cup bread crumbs
- ½ cup almond flour (almond meal)
- ¼ cup ground flaxseed

- 1 tbsp. Parmesan cheese, grated

sssssssssssssssssssssssssssssssssssssssssssss

**Procedure:**

**1:** Turn the oven to 350-degrees and let preheat. Prepare a 9x13 casserole dish by greasing the bottom.

**2:** Mix the eggs and yogurt together in a mixing bowl. In a second bowl, mix all the remaining ingredients (not including the chicken breasts).

**3:** Submerge each chicken breast into the eggs/yogurt mixture before dredging it through the dry mixture.

**4:** Place the coated chicken breasts in the casserole dish. Sprinkle the remaining bread crumb mixture over each of the breasts.

**5:** Bake the chicken breasts for 35 minutes. Serve the chicken immediately with your choice of a side, such as vegetables or a salad.

# 19) Vegetarian Casserole

This broccoli and cheese rice bake can be altered by adding cooked chicken if you want something more than a vegetarian meal.

**Yield:** 6

**Cooking Time:** 40 to 50 minutes

**List of Ingredients:**

- 2 pounds broccoli, chopped
- 1 cup brown rice, uncooked
- ½ onion, chopped
- 1 cup Greek yogurt, plain and nonfat
- 1 (14-ounce) can broth, vegetable
- ½ tsp. basil, ground
- 1 cup Cheddar cheese, divided in ¾ and ¼ cup
- 3 garlic cloves, minced
- 1 tbsp. bread crumbs

ssssssssssssssssssssssssssssssssssssssssssssssss

**Procedure:**

**1:** Preheat the oven to 350-degrees. Prepare a 1 ½-quart baking dish by greasing the bottom and sides.

**2:** Pour ¼ cup of water into a skillet. Place the skillet on the stove and bring the water to a boil. Add the onion and broccoli. Cover the skillet and let cook for about 3 minutes. You want the broccoli to be crunchy and brightly green. Set the skillet to the side for the moment.

**3:** In a large pot, add the broth and rice and bring to a boil. Cover the pot and reduce the heat to allow the mixture to simmer for about 20 minutes. You want the broth to be absorbed by the rice. Remove the pot from heat.

**4:** Add the basil, yogurt, garlic and ¾ cup of the cheddar cheese to the cooked rice. Stir until the mixture is well combined. Stir in the broccoli and onion from Step 2.

**5:** Transfer the rice mixture into the baking dish from Step 1. Sprinkle the bread crumbs and remaining cheese directly on top.

**6:** Place the dish in the oven and bake for 25 minutes. Serve warm with a side salad.

# 20) Zesty Mushroom Pork Chops

Made in a slow cooker, this zesty recipe can be altered to make more or less, depending on how many people you need to feed.

**Yield:** 6

**Cooking Time:** 25 to 30 minutes to prepare + 6 hours cooking

**List of Ingredients:**

- 6 pork chops
- 1 cup Greek yogurt, plain and nonfat
- ½ tsp. black pepper, ground
- ½ tsp. table salt
- ¼ tsp. paprika
- 1 tsp. garlic powder
- 2 tbsp. oil, vegetable or olive
- ½ cup flour, all-purpose
- 1 can chicken broth, low sodium
- 1 yellow onion, diced
- 8 ounces mushrooms, sliced
- ¼ cup vermouth

sssssssssssssssssssssssssssssssssssssssssssss

**Procedure:**

**1:** Mix the pepper, salt, paprika and garlic powder together in a small bowl. Season the pork chops with the mixture.

**2:** Drag the seasoned pork chops through the flour and set to the side.

**3:** Pour the oil into a large skillet. Set the skillet on the stove and heat the oil over medium heat. Place the seasoned and floured pork chops in the skillet.

**4:** Cook the pork chops for about 4 minutes on each side. You want the sides to get a nice brown color. Place the browned pork chops into the slow cooker.

**5:** Add the chopped onion directly on top of the pork chops and then carefully pour the chicken broth into the slow cooker. Turn the slow cooker on high and cook for 6 hours.

**6:** Remove the pork chops from the slow cooker and place on a plate. Transfer the broth mixture out of the slow cooker and into a skillet.

**7:** Place the mushrooms and vermouth into the broth-filled skillet and stir. Place the skillet over medium heat and cook for several minutes while stirring.

**8:** Remove the skillet from the stove and stir in the yogurt. Pour this mixture over the pork chops and serve while still warm.

# Chapter V: Desserts

ssssssssssssssssssssssssssssssssssssssssss

# 21) Vanilla Frozen Yogurt

This recipe is perfect for those hot summer days and, after one taste, you won't ever want to buy store-bought ice cream again!

**Yield:** 6

**Cooking Time:** 2 to 4 hours

**List of Ingredients:**

- 1 vanilla bean, halved and carefully scraped (2 tsp. of pure vanilla extract can be used as a substitute)
- 2 cups Greek yogurt, plain and low-fat
- ½ cup powdered sugar
- 2 tbsp. honey

sssssssssssssssssssssssssssssssssssssssssssss

**Procedure:**

**1:** In a large mixing bowl, mix all four ingredients together.

**2:** If mixing by hand, transfer the above mixture into a freezer-safe container. Seal the container tightly with the lid and let chill in the freezer for about 30 minutes. Remove the container from the freezer and mix with a fork. Place the container back into the freezer until the mixture becomes solid. Repeat the process of mixing with a fork every 30 minutes. Continue in this manner until the yogurt has frozen. Remove the container from the freezer and let sit on the counter for 5 minutes before dishing into bowls.

**3:** If you are going to use an ice cream maker, freeze the mixture according to the instructions of your specific ice cream maker.

## 22) Yogurt and Cream Cheese Frosting

This frosting works great on various cakes and tastes perfect when paired with the above carrot cake recipe.

**Yield:** 2 ½ cups of frosting

**Cooking Time:** 40 to 50 minutes

**List of Ingredients:**

- ½ cup Greek yogurt, plain and nonfat
- 2 tbsp. unsalted butter, softened
- ½ cup cream cheese, softened
- 1 ½ cups powdered sugar
- 1 tsp. vanilla extract

sssssssssssssssssssssssssssssssssssssssssssss

**Procedure:**

**1:** Use a stand or hand mixer to combine the yogurt, butter, cream cheese and vanilla together until smooth.

**2:** Gradually add the powdered sugar and mix until smooth.

**3:** Place the frosting in the fridge for at least 30 minutes. This will let the frosting thicken about before spreading.

# 23) Deliciously Light Cheesecake

This light take on the classic cheesecake recipes can be topped with fresh berries if desired.

**Yield:** 8

**Cooking Time:** 6 hours

**List of Ingredients:**

- ½ cup unsalted butter, melted
- 1 cup graham cracker crumbs
- 1 tbsp. + ¾ cup granulated sugar, divided
- ¼ tsp. cinnamon
- 1 cup Greek yogurt, plain and nonfat
- 1 (8-ounce) package cream cheese, softened
- 1 tbsp. vanilla extract
- 2 eggs
- 1 tbsp. lemon juice
- Berries, sliced (optional)

**Procedure:**

**1:** Preheat the oven to 325-degrees. Prepare a 9-inch pie pan by greasing the bottom and sides.

**2:** Mix the graham cracker crumbs, melted butter, 1 tbsp. sugar and cinnamon together in a small bowl. Press this mixture directly into the bottom and up the sides of the prepared pie pan. Place the pan in the oven and bake for 10 minutes.

**3:** In a mixing bowl, whisk the softened cream cheese, yogurt, ¾ cup sugar, lemon juice and vanilla extract together until smooth. Beat in the eggs one at a time until smooth.

**4:** Pour the cream cheese mixture into the pie pan. Place in the oven and bake for about 60 minutes or until the edges of the cheesecake develop a golden-brown color.

**5:** Let the cheesecake cool on a rake for about 30 minutes. Place the cake in the fridge and let chill for at least 4 hours. Add some sliced berries to the top of the cake and serve.

## 24) Carrot Yogurt Cake

Frost this delicious and easy-to-make carrot cake for the yogurt and cream cheese frosting (recipe found after this one).

**Yield:** 16

**Cooking Time:** 60 to 80 minutes

**List of Ingredients:**

- Flour, all-purpose (for coating the pan)
- 2 cups pastry flour, whole-wheat
- 1 ½ tsp. baking soda
- 2 tsp. baking powder
- ¼ tsp. table salt
- 2 tsp. cinnamon
- 3 large eggs, beaten
- 2 tsp. vanilla extract
- ¾ cup brown sugar, packed
- ¾ cup granulated sugar
- ½ cup unsweetened applesauce
- ½ cup grapeseed oil
- ½ cup Greek yogurt, plain and low-fat
- 2 cups carrots, shredded
- 1 (20-ounce) can crushed pineapple, drained
- ½ cups raisins (optional)
- ½ cup walnuts, chopped (optional)

sssssssssssssssssssssssssssssssssssssssssssss

**Procedure:**

**1:** Place the oven rack in the center of the oven. Turn the oven on and preheat to 350-degrees. Prepare a bundt pan by greasing it and then lightly coating it with all-purpose flour.

**2:** Mix the whole-wheat flour, baking soda, baking powder, salt and cinnamon together in a mixing bowl.

**3:** In a second mixing bowl, combine the brown sugar, granulated sugar, beaten eggs, vanilla extract, applesauce, oil and yogurt.

**4:** Fold the flour mixture into the sugar mixture until well combined. Add the shredded carrots, pineapple, raisins and walnuts and fold into the mixture.

**5:** Transfer the batter into the prepared bundt pan and place inside the oven. Bake for 45 minutes. Remove the cake from the oven and let cool completely before frosting.

# 25) White Chocolate Brownies

The yogurt in this recipe gives the brownies a soft texture.

**Yield:** 16

**Cooking Time:** 40 to 45 minutes

**List of Ingredients:**

- ¾ cup white sugar
- ½ cup butter, melted
- 1 tsp. vanilla extract
- 2 large eggs
- ¾ cup flour, all-purpose
- 1/3 cup cocoa powder, unsweetened
- ¼ tsp. salt
- ¼ tsp. baking salt
- ½ cup Greek yogurt, plain and nonfat
- ¾ cup white chocolate chips

ssssssssssssssssssssssssssssssssssssssssssssssss

**Procedure:**

**1:** Turn the oven to 350-degrees. Prepare an 8-inch baking pan by lightly coating the bottom of the pan with cooking spray.

**2:** Mix the sugar, butter, vanilla extract and eggs together until combined. In a separate bowl, shift the flour, cocoa, baking powder and salt together.

**3:** Slowly pour the flour mixture into the butter mixture and mix until well combined. Stir in the yogurt until it is incorporated into the mixture, but don't overmix it. Dump in the white chocolate chips and fold into the mixture.

**4:** Transfer the batter into the baking pan from Step 1. Place in the preheated oven and bake for about 30 minutes. You want a toothpick inserted into the center to come out clean. Let the bars cool before cutting into squares.

# About the Author

Allie Allen developed her passion for the culinary arts at the tender age of five when she would help her mother cook for their large family of 8. Even back then, her family knew this would be more than a hobby for the young Allie and when she graduated from high school, she applied to cooking school in London. It had always been a dream of the young chef to study with some of Europe's best and she made it happen by attending the Chef Academy of London.

After graduation, Allie decided to bring her skills back to North America and open up her own restaurant. After 10 successful years as head chef and owner, she decided to sell her business and pursue other career avenues. This monumental decision led Allie to her true calling, teaching. She also started to write e-books for her students to study at home for practice. She is now the proud author of several e-books and gives private and semi-private cooking lessons to a range of students at all levels of experience.

Stay tuned for more from this dynamic chef and teacher when she releases more informative e-books on cooking and baking in the near future. Her work is infused with stores and anecdotes you will love!

# Author's Afterthoughts

I can't tell you how grateful I am that you decided to read my book. My most heartfelt thanks that you took time out of your life to choose my work and I hope you find benefit within these pages.

There are so many books available today that offer similar content so that makes it even more humbling that you decided to buying mine.

Tell me what you thought! I am eager to hear your opinion and ideas on what you read as are others who are looking for a good book to buy. Leave a review on Amazon.com so others can benefit from your wisdom!

*With much thanks,*

*Allie Allen*

Printed in Great Britain
by Amazon